PRAISE

Faith Begins at Home
GRANDPARENTS

Outside of mom and dad, grandparents are the people most likely to lead a young boy or girl to faith in Jesus Christ. Mark Holmen offers a wonderful primer to help grandparents embrace this awesome and wonderful privilege.

Jim Daly
President, Focus on the Family

There has never been a more important time for grandparents to play a significant role in the life and faith development of their families. All studies show that a grandparent's influence in the life of his or her grandchildren is extremely significant. Mark Holmen is one of the central figures and leaders in helping families thrive spiritually around the world. This booklet is beautifully written and incredibly practical. Grandparents finally have a wonderful resource to help them impact the faith of their family.

Jim Burns, Ph.D
President, HomeWord
Author, *Faith Conversations for Families* and *Confident Parenting*

Every generation benefits from leaders who challenge it to reach for excellence. Mark's life experiences have equipped him to be an insightful leader who calls readers to action. His message is powerful and simple: We need more "faith at home." I hope to hear Mark proclaim this message for many years to come. I thoroughly endorse and support him in his vision to establish "faith at home" in households around the world!

Ken Canfield, Ph.D.
Founder, National Center for Fathering

In many families, the generations are fragmented and disconnected—and the forces of evil could not be happier. It is time for a grandparenting reformation! This book is filled with encouragement, biblical vision and practical ways you can impact the generations of your family for Christ

Dr. Rob Rienow

Founder, Visionary Family Ministries
www.VisionaryFam.com

Mark Holmen

Author, *Faith Begins at Home* and Founder of Faith @ Home Ministries

Faith Begins @Home GRAND PARENTS

BETHANYHOUSE

a division of Baker Publishing Group
Minneapolis, Minnesota

© 2014 by Mark Holmen

Published by Bethany House Publishers
11400 Hampshire Avenue South
Bloomington, Minnesota 55438
www.bethanyhouse.com

Bethany House Publishers is a division of
Baker Publishing Group, Grand Rapids, Michigan

Bethany House edition published 2015
ISBN 978-0-7642-1490-5

Previously published by Regal Books

Printed in the United States of America

All rights reserved. No part of this publication may be reproduced,
stored in a retrieval system, or transmitted in any form or by any
means—for example, electronic, photocopy, recording—without the
prior written permission of the publisher. The only exception is brief
quotations in printed reviews.

Library of Congress Control Number: 2015948915

Scripture quotations are from the Holy Bible, New International Ver-
sion®. NIV®. Copyright © 1973, 1978, 1984 by Biblica, Inc.™ Used
by permission of Zondervan. All rights reserved worldwide.

This book is dedicated to the memory of my mom, Myrne Jeannette Holmen, who was tragically killed in a car accident in May of 2013. She was taking her normal weekly journey to a nearby town to run errands when a semitruck ran through a stop sign leaving her no where to go but to collide into the side of his truck. She battled violently for eight days before she went to be with the Lord on May 2 of 2013. I was able to be with her, holding her hand, as she took her last breath—something for which I will always be grateful.

My mom was the epitome of Faith@Home and I wouldn't be the missionary, husband, father, pastor, speaker or writer that I am without her constant unconditional love and steady encouraging and supportive influence. If you wanted to see a Faith@Home person you needed to look no further than Myrne Holmen as spending just five minutes with her would leave you feeling blessed and encouraged. One of the greatest examples of this was showcased by the people who attended her celebration of life service that included not only family and friends, but everyday people who were influenced by her, including the pharmacy workers, local gallery owners who closed their store to attend, bank attendants and her favorite waitress!

If the ministry of Faith @Home or this book is a blessing to you then you have two people to thank; our Lord and Savior Jesus Christ and my mom Myrne Holmen. A designated fund has been established in her memory that will be used to underwrite international and/or urban ministry Faith@Home outreach events or seminars. My mom had a passion to see the Faith@Home message spread both internationally and into urban environments. She always wished she could travel with me on many of my international trips. If you would like to give a love offering to Faith@Home Ministries, in honor of Myrne Holmen to spread the Faith@Home message into urban and international environments, simply make your check payable to Faith@Home Ministries (the MJH Fund) and mail it to 37483 Deer Ridge Drive, Crosslake, MN 56442. Thank you.

Contents

Introduction

One of the blessings of being a pastor and speaker is connecting with so many wonderful people across the country and world. It seems that each time I speak, preach or lead a seminar I will have a few individuals come up to me and share an experience that they have had with implementing some sort of faith at home principle with their children or grandchildren. Over the years I have had the opportunity to write numerous books for parents where I have been able to utilize some of those stories and insights.

- *Faith Begins at Home*
- *Faith Begins@Home Mom*—my wife Maria wrote this one
- *Faith Begins@Home Dad*
- *Faith Begins@Home Prayer*
- *Faith Begins@Home Devotions*
- *Faith Begins@Home Family*
- *Impress Faith on Your Kids*

Over the past three years I have seen a greater number of grandparents coming to my parenting seminars seeking wisdom or tips from me for how to become a greater spiritual influence in the lives of their adult children and grandchildren. Their participation has opened my eyes to the realities they face and it has given me a chance to hear some of their wonderful stories, experiences and examples. This book gives me a chance to delve into the topic of being a faith at home focused grandparent who is actively engaged in the faith formation of children and grandchildren and to share some of the wonderful insights and ideas I have collected over the years. So whether you are a first-time or long-time grandparent, grandparent-to-be or grandparent-type person who is an aunt, uncle, godparent, etc., who is interested in discovering practical ways to become a strong spiritual influence in the lives of children, then this book is for you!

1-2 Knockout Punch

I recently received a phone call from my sister. She excitedly shared with me the following: "Mark, I just got a call from Noah and his wife asking me if I would be the godmother for their newborn daughter." My sister, at the time, was a fifty-three-old single woman who had been a long time friend for Noah and his parents. Yet it still came as quite a surprise to her when she was asked to be the godmother. "I'm so excited that they want me to play a role in their daughter's life, and yet I'm wondering what I should do? What does it mean to be godmother?"

Thankfully, this was not the first time I had been asked this question. However, when it is your sister, you always feel a little more pressure to come through with a good answer. I simply shared with her the following advice. "You have been given a huge opportunity to be a long-term spiritual influence in the life of this child. One simple thing you can do is to make the anniversary date of your godchild's dedication/infant baptism a special date between you and her. Celebrate this date every year by sending her a spiritual gift just as you would send her a birthday gift on her birthday. As she grows older continue to utilize this day as a time to take her to dinner or a movie and continue to pour spiritual wisdom and gifts into her life. Claim the dedication/infant baptism date as your day to spoil her spiritually with gifts and/or resources that will help her grow in her relationship with Jesus Christ." When I finished speaking, you could hear the relief in my sister's voice as she said, "Now that's something I can do and I'm going to do it!"

When Gospel Light and I agreed on this book, a part of me was wondering if I was qualified to write it. I'm not a grandparent yet and don't plan to be one for a while as my daughter is only seventeen (did you hear that Malyn?). Yet in spite of these misgivings, I felt clearly called by God to write this booklet based on the number of grandparents I have encountered and talked to over my years in ministry, first as a pastor and then as a missionary to the Faith@Home movement. I pray this booklet will be a blessing not only to grandparents, but grandparents-to-be, aunts, uncles and anyone who is in a "grandparent-type" position or role in the life of a child. I'm targeting this book to you.

'   One of the studies that changed my life and perspective was the Significant Religious Influences survey from Effective Christian Education: A National

Study of Protestant Congregations by Search Institute.[1] The purpose of this survey was to identify
the people and things that influence children to
have faith in Christ. The top two influencers were
mom and dad, but guess what number three was?
Grandparents! Numerous studies have been done
since and they confirm these findings which, if you
think about it, make grandparents the most influential people when it comes to passing on faith to the
next generations. Why are grandparents the most influential? First and foremost they are still mom and
dad, which means they maintain that primary influ-
encer role in the lives of their children even when they
are adults. Then as grandparents they are the next
most influential people in the faith formation of children. So in many ways, if we want the Christian faith
to be passed on to the next generations, grandparents
are a critical key component to this happening.

One of the things I have seen over my past 20+
years in ministry is the fact that many "grandparent-
type" people are disengaging from being an influence
in the faith formation of their children and children's
children and there are two primary reasons for this.
These reasons are a "1-2 Knockout Punch" because
these two things knock more grandparents and
grandparent-type individuals out of the spiritual
influence game than anything else.

First, for many, the primary reason why they are
not engaged in the spiritual formation of their grandchildren is guilt. Many grandparent-type people have

guilt because they feel they didn't do well enough by their own children, therefore, they have no right to engage in the spiritual lives of their grandchildren.

> Pastor Mark, I blew it with my kids. I was the biggest hypocrite in the world. I took my kids to church on Sunday and made sure they were involved in all the programs of the church, but I never set an example for them through my own life. I never prayed with them, read the Bible with them or engaged in a faith talk with them. For them Christianity was something we did at church but that was pretty much where it ended and now they have walked away from Christianity. How can I possibly engage in my grandchildren's lives when I failed with my children? How can I do something with my grandchildren that I didn't do with my own kids?

This is a common testimony I have heard from hundreds of grandparents and the following is a story of a situation where I was forced to give a response to this concern.

I'll never forget the day when I was asked to speak to our Seniors Sunday School class on the Sunday when they were having an event entitled, "How to Be a Meddling Grandparent." The purpose of the event was to inspire and motivate grandparent-type people to take a more active role in the faith formation of their children and children's children. The pastor to seniors, Jim, asked me to open the event, but not being a grandparent I wasn't sure what he wanted me to say. "Pastor Mark," Jim shared, "you know our seniors support you and your passionate vision for faith at home. One thing I think you need to be aware of is the fact that for many of us your passion for seeing parents take a more active role in the faith formation of their children brings up a point of pain. Many in our seniors community were not very engaged in the faith formation of their children and as a result they have seen sons and daughters walk away from the faith. That now causes great concern. So while we support your vision for faith at home, for many it is a sensitive topic and we are wondering where this message and emphasis was 30 years ago."

I appreciated Jim sharing this insight with me, and knowing what the seniors were feeling gave me time to prepare and seek God's will for what I would say.

"I have been informed that while you love and support our faith at home focus, for many of you this emphasis brings up a point of pain. You have children who have walked away from the faith and now you are wondering if maybe what you did and what you didn't do at home, is a big part of the reason why. The guilt you are carrying over the fact that your children have walked away from their Christian faith today has you feeling you cannot be an influence in the lives of your grandchildren because this would come across as hypocritical to your adult children."

You could have heard a pin drop. I had clearly hit a nerve. I then continued with the words God had laid on my heart. "I'm sorry if you have children who have walked away from the faith; and I'm sorry if the church did not equip you to be the faith at home focused type of parents you were called to be. I'm sorry this message and emphasis wasn't here for you 30 years ago. That is our fault as a church, not yours. So on behalf of the church I'm asking for your forgiveness. Will you forgive us for failing you as parents?"

The reaction I received was pretty overwhelming. You could see heads raise and eyes move from looking at the floor to looking directly at me. I waited and then I repeated the question. "Will you forgive us for not focusing enough of our time, energy and resources when you were a parent by relentlessly inspiring, motivating and equipping you to be the primary spiritual influence in the life of your children? I confess to you that as a church we probably got too caught up in building buildings and starting programs and we lost sight of the fact that the home, and what you do with your children there, is more influential in shaping their faith than anything we do here at church. As you can see we are not going to forget that anymore. It is the reason why we have made a commitment to being a faith at home focused church. That doesn't negate the fact we failed you when you needed us to do this for you. So again, please hear me when I say that I am sorry. Will you forgive us?"

There was complete silence until one gentleman responded, "It's okay, Pastor, you don't need to apologize. The fact that you acknowledge this means a lot. It shows that you truly understand where we are coming from. Plus it was the previous pastor's fault anyway!" After a few other people commented, I then turned my attention to the conclusion of my message which had the following challenge for them. "*Okay*, now that forgiveness has been granted, it is time for you to get over your guilt, by recognizing God gives his grace. It's time for you to get back in the game because you are still moms and dads as well as grandparents and you are still more influential than anything the church or anyone else can do to lead your grandchildren into a growing relationship with Christ. Satan knows that. That is why he is working so hard, utilizing guilt, to get you out of the game. You need to realize there is no retirement plan for passing on the faith to our children and children's children. It's time to get back in the game!"

• •

Grandparents do not let guilt keep them out of the game as spiritual influencers.

• •

The second reason I have seen for why many grandparent-type people do not engage in the faith formation of their children or children's children is what I would simply describe as fear. Fear over the fact that they don't want to meddle too much, overdo it or come across as too pushy. Fear over the fact that they're not sure if what they want to do will really work or not. Fear that what they are thinking of doing will be considered outdated, dumb, not cool or old fashioned.

It's amazing how many reasons we can come up with for not being a spiritual influence in the lives of our children and children's children. We'll talk about that more in a later chapter. They include things like:

- I'm not old enough, progressive enough or close enough to do it.
- I haven't been married nor do I have children of my own so how can I be a grandparent-type influence?
- I blew it with my kids so I would come across as a huge hypocrite if I tried to engage in the spiritual lives of my grandchildren.
- I don't know how to text, email, tweet, post, etc. so I don't think I can relate to them in the way they need me to.

I want you to know that all of these are lies from Satan, the father of lies. Satan realizes how influential you are as a mom, dad, grandparent, godparent, aunt, uncle, etc. and Satan wants to get you off the playing field. He is using guilt and fear as his primary weapons. Don't fall for Satan's lies. It doesn't matter who you are, what you've done or not done or where you live, God has brought you into relationship with your children and your children's children for a reason. You need to trust that God can and will use you and not let guilt and fear keep you out of the game. Don't let Satan get a double win, the first win through guilt for what you did or didn't do with your own kids, and the second win through fear that keeps you disengaged from your children and grandchildren's lives. "It is for freedom that Christ has set us free. Stand firm, then, and do not let yourselves be burdened again by a yoke of slavery" (Galatians 5:1). You need to recognize that God's grace covers *all* of your past transgressions and failings and you have been restored completely, so there is nothing stopping you from being the influence God has called and equipped you to be in the lives of your children and your children's children. God can and will do great and wonderful things through you so you need to cast aside all the fears you may have and put your trust completely in Him who will give you strength, wisdom and everything you need.

But now, this is what the LORD says—he who created you, Jacob [insert your name here], he who formed you, Israel [insert your name here]: Do not fear, for I have redeemed you; I have summoned you by name; you are mine. When you pass through the waters, I will be with you; and when you pass through the rivers, they will not sweep over you. When

> you walk through the fire, you will not be
> burned; the flames will not set you ablaze.
> For I am the LORD your God (Isaiah 43:1-3)

I don't know who you are, where you are or how this book ended up in your hands, but I do trust in a God, Father/Son/Holy Spirit, who is continually working in ways that we will never know, see or understand. I am trusting that He has put this book in your hands for a reason. You may or may not be a grandparent. You may be a godparent, aunt, uncle or simply a family friend, and yet you are in a position of influence in the life of a child. You may be feeling overwhelmed or excited, ready or completely ill prepared. It really doesn't matter because you have been called for such a time as this to be an influence in the life of a child. There are a lot of things to fear and yet God is with you, so don't let fear keep you from wading into the waters or walking into the flames. God is with you! The question now becomes what type of influence will you be? You can't avoid it; you are going to influence one way or another. Will you lead those in your life towards or away from Christ? What you have done or not done up to this point no longer matters. You serve a God of grace and second chances. My prayer is that through the remaining pages of this book you will receive the guidance and direction you need to be a long-term spiritual influence in the life of a child, because, at the end of the day, there is simply nothing better than this.

DISCUSSION QUESTIONS

1. Who were your primary spiritual influencers?
2. What role did grandparents, godparents, aunts, uncles or other grandparent-type people play in your spiritual journey?
3. Are you carrying any guilt over the way you spiritually nurtured your children? If you had it a do over, what would you do differently?
4. What fears do you have today that are keeping you from being a spiritual influence in the lives of your children and grandchildren? What's something you would like to try?

Note
1. Search Institute is a nonprofit, nonsectarian research and educational organization that advances the wellbeing and positive development of children and youth through applied research, evaluation, consultation, training and the development of publications and practical resources for educators, youth-serving professionals, parents, community leaders and policy makers. Phone: 1-800-888-7828. Website: www.search-institute.org.

2

Influencing the
Influencers

I will never forget the comment Charles Barkley (at the time an NBA superstar) made that got him into a lot of trouble. "I am not a role model," he said. The reason he said it was because he didn't like being challenged by reporters about his behavior and the impact it would make on the thousands of kids who looked up to him as their role model, so he simply responded, "I am not a role model." In reality Charles Barkley did not want to be a role model because he didn't like the idea of having to live up to the standards that went with being a role model. However, because of his stature and popularity, he *was* a role model to thousands of kids whether he wanted to be or not. Thankfully, most of us do not have to live under the spotlight that professional athletes do. The fact remains that if you are a grandparent, godparent, aunt, uncle or adoptive grandparent you are a role model whether you want to be or not. There is no way around it. You can't escape it and the question becomes what are you going to do with that responsibility and opportunity?

It's a responsibility—In Hebrew thought and practice, from which most of our Old Testament comes, it is important to note that among Israelites three generations often lived in one home. The grandfather was usually the religious head, primarily because he was the elder of the household. Grandparents stayed intimately engaged in the lives of their descendants for as many generations as they lived to see. There was no attitude of "I'll leave the training to the parents" as there is no specific word for "grandfather" or "grandmother" in Hebrew. That meant that every command of Scripture given to fathers was also a command to grandfathers regarding their grandchildren. Therefore, passing on the faith from one generation to the next was an intergenerational responsibility and normal expectation for grandparents. It was clearly a part of God's plan all along.

• •

Do you feel it is your responsibility to pass on the faith to as many generations as you live to see in your family, or have you abdicated that responsibility to the parents or the church?

• •

It's an opportunity!—I remember my father telling me, "Every responsibility is an opportunity." From that I learned to see responsibilities as blessings not burdens. You have an opportunity to influence the lives of children of multiple generations and that's not a burden, it's a blessing. That's what makes it so grand! There is a reason they call it *grand* parenting because you have grander wisdom and experience to draw from simply because you have lived a longer life than parents and children have. You also have a grander opportunity to influence multiple generations of people which only someone at your stage in life can do. The longer you live, the more generations you have the opportunity to influence. Your potential to be used by God only increases with age. As one grandparent told me, "Whether I like to admit it or not, I'm old, so I might as well use it to my advantage because it's about the only advantage I have left!"

. . . .

Are you seizing the opportunity you have been given to influence the lives of the generations that follow you to follow Christ?

. . . .

A Biblical Example

Throughout the Bible we see God use grandparent-type individuals to speak wisdom and truth to His people. One of those examples can be found in the book of Joshua. Towards the end of the book of Joshua, in chapter 24, we are given Joshua's farewell message to the leaders of Israel. We are told that now

Joshua is "old and well advanced in years" (Joshua 23:1, *ESV*). The Bible goes on to say that, "Joshua assembled all the tribes [sometimes translated families] of Israel at Shechem. He summoned the elders, leaders, judges and officials of Israel, and they presented themselves before God" (Joshua 24:1).

Essentially, all people of influence had been gathered together and through this message Joshua was imparting wisdom that would "influence the influencers." As grandparents you are in a position to influence multiple generations. What should you be influencing as a Faith@Home grandparent and how should you go about doing it?

Influence Them to Remember

When you read the first thirteen verses of Joshua's farewell address in chapter 24 you see that Joshua begins by recalling all the things that God has done for the people of Israel. It is clear that Joshua does not want them to forget who their God is and what their God has done for them. One of my favorite passages, that comes from the book just before Joshua, is another instruction from Moses to the people of Israel where he states, "When the LORD your God brings you into the land he swore to your fathers, to Abraham, Isaac and Jacob, to give you—a land with large, flourishing cities you did not build, houses filled with all kinds of good things you did not provide, wells you did not dig, and vineyards and olive groves you did not plant—then when you eat and are satisfied, *be careful that you do not forget the LORD, who brought you out of Egypt, out of the land of slavery"* (Deuteronomy 6:10-12, emphasis added). One of the dangers for families today is that they get so busy "doing life" that they forget the One who has given them the life that they have. Moses was warning the people that they will be inheriting a land of plenty, which is great, but it can also lead them to forget God if they are not careful. Joshua, in his farewell address picks up on this theme and begins by reminding the people, again, of who their God is and all the things God has done for them which I would paraphrase as follows:

- Remember how God led you.
- Remember how God provided for you.
- Remember how God sent people into your life.
- Remember how God delivered you.
- Remember how God destroyed those who tried to destroy you.
- Remember that God gave you "land on which you did not toil and cities you did not build; and you live in them and eat from vineyards and olive groves that you did not plant" (Joshua 24:13).

As grandparents, the first thing you can do is to make sure that the generations that are behind you do not forget who God is and what God has done for us. As grandparents you need to tell the God story again and again, whether you think they know it or not, so that they won't forget God. And as you do, be sure to personalize it as well. You have a story of how God has led you, provided for you, sent people into your life, delivered you and even destroyed those who have tried to hurt you. Make sure your children know that story because remembering who God is and what God has done for us makes us fall in love with Him all over again.

. . . .

Take some time to write your God story out so that your children and children's children can know it and have a copy of it. Use the format from Joshua as your guide; as you look back over your life recall and write down how God has led you, provided for you, sent people into your life, delivered you, destroyed those who tried to hurt you, and given you what you have been given? Read it and give it to your family at Christmas or on their birthday.

. . . .

Influence Them to Fear

We live in a world where we are taught to fear nothing and yet throughout Scripture we are told to "fear and love God." In verse 14 Joshua admonishes the people when he says, "Now fear the LORD and serve him with all faithfulness" (Joshua 24:14). When you are young you don't know what fear is or what to fear. How many times have you seen a toddler reach out to touch a hot oven? They simply don't know what fear is, yet the longer you live, the more your fear increases because you know more of what exists that needs to be feared. You can see this in Joshua's farewell message where just a few verses earlier he shares the following with the people. "Now I am about to go the way of all the earth. You know with all your heart and soul that not one of all the good promises the LORD your God gave you has failed. Every promise has been fulfilled; not one has failed. But just as every good promise of the LORD your God has come true, so the LORD will bring on you all the evil he has threatened, until he has destroyed you from this good land he has given you. If you violate the covenant of the LORD your God, which he commanded you, and go and serve other gods and bow down to them, the LORD's anger will burn against you, and you will quickly perish from the good land he has given you" (Joshua 23:14-16).

Now no one likes to hear about "the Lord's anger burning against you" or that we could "quickly perish from the good land he has given," but as grandparents, I'm sure you can attest to the fact that what Joshua is saying here is absolutely true. The fact of the matter is that there are things we should be afraid of, including living outside the will and commands of God. I have had hundreds of grandparents come to me with tears in their eyes expressing fear over the fact that their children and grandchildren are not walking with the Lord. The longer you live the more you realize that death could come at any moment and that those who give their life to Christ and follow

Him will live eternally, while those who don't will perish. We don't want our kids or grandchildren to perish and yet we fearfully realize it could happen at any moment and there's nothing we can do about it and that is scary and something we should fear.

Appropriate fear is not a bad thing; in fact it's a very important thing. Appropriate fear keeps us from doing stupid and destructive things. I'm afraid of cliffs and as a result I don't go near a cliff and that keeps me from falling off and dying. I'm also afraid every time my daughter drives away that it might be the last time I see her on this side of heaven. Yet fear doesn't paralyze me it drives me. It drives me away from cliffs and towards making sure my daughter, and one day her children if we are so blessed, realize that death and destruction is real and could happen at any moment in time, yet it doesn't have to be the end of the story. Through Christ, and what he did for us on the cross, it can be defeated. Fear should drive us to Christ, and as grandparents, it is your responsibility and opportunity to help your children and children's children know what to fear as you know that better than anyone.

Influence Them to Serve with All Faithfulness

As the age-old adage goes, "actions speak louder than words" and if you were to ask me what I have seen as the greatest thing grandparents can do to influence their children and children's children to follow Christ I would simply say, "Serve Him with *all* faithfulness." Your actions, in how you joyfully and obediently serve the Lord, will speak more to your children and grandchildren than anything you can say. And as a person of influence, what you say and do matters, and that's why the passage reads, "with *all* faithfulness." This isn't something you can do part time nor is there a retirement plan for your faithful service to God. You need to show how to forgive with all faithfulness, love with all faithfulness, restore with all faithfulness, persevere with all faithfulness, trust with all faithfulness and obey with all faithfulness. This will influence them to see that faithfulness is a lifestyle that is lived rather than simply a church service you begrudgingly go to once a week. Remember, your kids and grandkids will in all likelihood grow to love and serve what you love and serve. Influence them to love and serve Him by you loving and serving Him with *all* faithfulness.

Influence Them to Choose

Probably the most recognized and recited portion of Joshua's farewell message is his quote, "Choose for yourselves this day whom you will serve. . . as for me and my household, we will serve the LORD" (Joshua 24:15). Our children and grandchildren make decisions every day and those decisions are influenced by others. The critical question becomes, are you one of their influencers?" I love how Joshua handled the way in which he would influence them to choose. He started by acknowledging the choices/options that they had. There were other gods they could worship and serve and he wasn't shying away from that reality. Therefore a good starting point, when it comes to helping others make decisions, is to start by asking, "What are all the options?" This is a disarming first step because it allows them to share with you the things they are considering and it keeps the focus on them and the choice they have to make rather than on you. Then Joshua asks them to consider what the Lord might want them to do. I call this the WWJHYD moment. Many of you may remember the famous WWJD bracelets which stood for What Would Jesus Do. While I liked that statement I always had a little bit of a problem with it because I could easily dismiss it by saying, "Well Jesus would part the sea here and I can't do that because I'm not Jesus." Yet when I added two words to it everything changed for me. Instead of What Would Jesus Do I changed it to What Would Jesus Have You Do? When Joshua confronted the people with his statement, "but if serving the Lord seems undesirable to you" this seems to indicate that they had been challenged to consider what the Lord would have wanted them to do. So as a second step, after you have asked them what the options are, you may simply want to ask "What would God want you to do?" or "Where do you feel God is leading you?" Again, these are disarming questions that put the focus back on them and what God might be saying to them. Then Joshua simply shared the choice he would make; "As for me and my household we will serve the

Lord." As a person of influence, after hearing the options and helping them to consider what God would want them to do, you have the right and opportunity to share your opinion, but be sure to phrase it, "As for me . . ." It is your opinion and perspective only but at the end of the day you are not the decision maker, they are. It is their choice and they are going to have to live with the consequences. You can, however, influence and you have that responsibility and opportunity as a grandparent.

Influence Them to Stay True

After Joshua had concluded his message and the people had made a commitment to follow his lead in serving and obeying God with their lives, Joshua did one final thing. "On that day Joshua made a covenant for the people, and there at Shechem he drew up for them decrees and laws. And Joshua recorded these things in the Book of the Law of God. Then he took a large stone and set it up there under the oak near the holy place of the LORD. 'See!' he said to all the people. 'This stone will be a witness against us. It has heard all the words the LORD has said to us. It will be a witness against you if you are untrue to your God'" (Joshua 24:25-27). Joshua found a way that he could still influence them, even from the grave, to remain followers of God through a symbolic rock that was placed in a place of prominence where the people would consistently see it.

I was asked to give the message at a funeral of a man who had been a "Joshua type" lifelong follower of

Christ. His name was Ray and he had a family with multiple generations of Christ followers as a result of his faithfulness and influence which made the funeral an extra special occasion. As I prepared the message the Holy Spirit gave me a theme for his message that was WYSWYG & WWJHYD because Ray was a "What You See is What You Get" type of guy, not perfect by any means but a man who lived his life consistently according to "What Would Jesus Have You Do?" I knew Ray would not want my message to be boring or sad but that he would like it to be celebratory with some sort of uniqueness to it. With the theme in mind, I ordered bracelets with WYSWYG and WWJHMD on them and at the conclusion of my message I talked about how Ray's influence will continue to influence us and then I handed out the bracelets so that everyone could remember what God had taught all of us through Ray. As grandparents you may want to find symbolic ways or things you can give to your children or grandchildren that will help them to remember those things you want them to remember.

DISCUSSION QUESTIONS

1. Who were some of your role models/influencers growing up? Who do you turn to today for advice/counsel?
2. Which convicts you more, the responsibility of being a grandparent or the opportunity?

3. Of the four ways to influence: Influence Them to Remember, Influence Them to Fear, Influence Them to Serve, Influence Them to Stay True, which one do you need to work on the most?

4. How can you go about being a better influence? What are some specific things you can do?

3

Overcoming Roadblocks

As I prepared to write this book I posted a question on my Twitter and Facebook pages that simply asked, "What are some of the roadblocks you face as a grandparent in being a spiritual influence in the life of your grandchildren?" I was surprised with the quantity and quality of responses I received. As I sifted through the responses, the following became the most consistently identified roadblocks of the comments I received.

Roadblock #1–Distance

Far and away, no pun intended, distance was identified as the primary roadblock that is preventing many grandparents from engaging in the spiritual lives of their grandchildren:

> Distance is a hindrance. My parents live 1,000 miles away, my husband's parents live out of town as well, so I would be interested (as I

know they would be) in some ideas on how to foster that relationship long distance.

I wish we could be more of a spiritual influence in the lives of our grandchildren but we live over 2,000 miles apart and I only see them once or twice a year for the holidays or some sort of short visit as they are passing through. I really wish I could be more of an influence in their lives but I'm not sure what I can do being this far apart from them.

There is no way around the fact that we live in a mobile society where home is wherever your job, or spouse, takes you. I will never forget the day we had to tell our families who lived in Minnesota and Iowa that we were going to be moving from Minneapolis, Minnesota to take a call serving as the Senior Pastor of a church in Ventura, California. While this alone would be difficult news to share, what made it even more difficult was the fact that, at the time, we were taking the only grandchild/niece, who was only six years old with us. While both of our families supported our decision, everyone knew that the distance between us was certainly going to change things. And it did. My sisters, parents, and in-laws were the only babysitters my daughter had ever had, but that had to change. Weekends, or even evenings, with our families happened on a relatively frequent basis, but that would change as our times together would now need to be coordinated and even budgeted for rather than simply being spontaneous. The distance clearly changed things and yet, in spite of the distance, we found ways to remain families that are still closely connected. My daughter's aunts, uncle and grandparents remain an influence in her life.

Here are some roadblock busters to help you break through the distance roadblock.

Roadblock Busters

- *Utilize Technology to Close the Gap*: While we may want to complain about the way technology is constantly changing and updating, which we have every right to do, the good news is that in an upwardly mobile society we have technology that can be utilized to keep us close. As a writer and speaker I do a lot of national and international traveling which takes me away from my wife and daughter, yet through Skype, text messaging, Facebook posts and even Facetime we can communicate to each other multiple times a day. Many times, I find my communication with my daughter improves when I'm gone as sometimes I get more out of her through texting than I would if I was trying to have a conversation with her in our home. If you are a grandparent where distance separates you from your kids and grandchildren, I would strongly encourage you to utilize technology to close the distance gap. You don't have to miss out on what they are experiencing or going through because in all likelihood they have posted it somewhere that you can access! Engage with your children and grandchildren through regular cell phone conversations or Skype calls if they live outside the U.S. Utilize text messaging to send them a Scripture verse, blessing or prayer request. Get a Facebook page and post things on their Facebook pages. Follow them on Twitter or Foursquare and if you don't know what these things are or how to do this . . . *ask them to help you!* When my mom first started texting my daughter she would come running to me saying, "Dad, I just got another text from Nana. Let's try to decipher it!" Clearly, my mom was not very good at texting because of those "darn little old buttons," and yet her effort impressed my daughter and made her love her Nana even more for trying. So please hear me when I say, you won't be as good as your grandchildren are when it comes to technology, but you don't have to be. Just trying will make a difference and don't tell me you can't stay connected with your grandchildren, because you can. We live in a world that makes it easy so take advantage of it.

- *Write Letters*: Another way to close the distance gap is to simply write letters to your grandchildren. My daughter is 17 and I could probably count on one hand how many personal letters she has received over her lifetime other than cards on holidays. It seems like the only mail we get today is junk mail which makes personal letters all the more exciting and appealing to receive. The only "real" letters my daughter received were from my mom, and now that my mom has gone to be with the Lord those letters continue to be an influence in my daughter's life—she keeps them in the top drawer of her desk at home. If anything, I wish my mom would have written her, and me for that matter, more letters!

- *Visit Them (or Pay Them to Visit You!)*: Let me tread lightly here, but one of the things I have seen surface in many grandparents is the not so spiritual gift of stubbornness. (Yes, mom, this was even true about you—but don't strike me down for it!) It's as if many have taken it personally that their kids have moved away and so out of spite, towards no one in particular, they are simply going to sit at home stubbornly saying, "I wish I could see my grandkids more." My simple response is this, *Get off your duff and go!* Buy the tickets, talk to your doctor and get the medications you will need, find someone to watch your house and pets, take some of that money you have in savings, get past whatever issues you have with traveling, and go! Quit being stubborn and quit coming up with excuses and even if your last visit wasn't the best, it doesn't mean the next one can't be better. You have the time and availability to visit them, so make it happen. Or if you are not in a position to do that, offer to pay to have your family come to you. Trust me that will be a good investment that will bear fruit for years to come.

Roadblock #2–Apprehension that Their Parents Will Not Approve

Many shared that the primary reason they did not engage in the spiritual lives of their grandchildren was due to the fact they did not feel it would be welcomed or appreciated by the parents:

> I know that my mom has talked to me about the difficulty of influencing my sister's family because of the boundaries that my sister set in the type of relationship Mom could have with the grandchildren.

> In my own family, my parents have been apprehensive because they were unsure of what we would be "comfortable" with.

What prevents us the most from engaging more in grandchildren's lives is a strong belief on the part of one of the parents that only he/she can have any say in the spiritual life of the child. I just try to be patient and as much as I can exhibit a spiritual life. And take opportunities as they come up!

In working with hundreds of grandparents it seems that many do not engage in the spiritual lives of their grandchildren because they are worried that the parents will feel they are being too pushy. They don't want to do anything that would prevent the parents from allowing them to spend time with their grandchildren. I understand, and I think it is important that grandparents be sensitive to and honoring of the parents. But that doesn't have to paralyze you or mean you can't do anything. Instead, it creates an opportunity.

Roadblock Busters
I think there is a simple three-step process you can follow that will help you get past the fear and/or apprehension you may have with your grandchildren's parents.

- *Step 1—Figure Out What You Want to Do:* Instead of worrying about what your grandchildren aren't experiencing, focus your attention on what you would like to introduce to them. How would you like to influence them? Do you want to pray with them at mealtime?

Do you want to read the Bible to them? Do you want to take them to church? What is it that you would like them to know or experience about what it means to be a Christian?

- *Step 2—Ask Permission:* Find a time or opportunity to tell the parents what you would like to do or experience with your grandchildren and why you would like to do this. (It's is important for them to see your heart/passion for why this is important to you.) Get their permission/approval. If you get approval great! If not, tweak your plan/idea and try again.
- *Step 3—Follow Through and Give Thanks:* Now that you have been given the green light, then follow through fully with the things you have been given permission to do. After doing so, be sure to send a note of thanks to the parents for their willingness to allow you to do these things.

One set of grandparents I talked with were worried about their grandchildren, and the fact that they were not being raised with any form of Christian influence in their home. So they reached an agreement with the parents, that included their son, that they would not bring any "Jesus stuff" into their home environment, but when the grandchildren came to stay at their house it was permissible for Nana and Papa to pray and read the Bible with the children and even take them to church. A few years later the grandparents asked their son and daughter-in-law if they could purchase a week of Bible camp for their granddaughter for her birthday. The parents agreed without hesitation. The grandparents knew a week of Bible camp could be a huge and lasting spiritual experience for their granddaughter, and they also knew that their son and daughter-in-law would appreciate a week with one less child in the house—which turned out to be the case. These grandparents had an intentional yet adaptable plan for how they were going to influence their grandchildren to know, love and follow Christ, and yet they made sure to honor the parents in the way they implemented their plan. By doing this, instead of making their son and daughter-in-law feel guilty for what they weren't doing, they instead praised them for what the parents allowed them to do, and that only strengthened the grandparents' relationship with the parents.

Roadblock #3–Unresolved Parent/Child Conflict

Another roadblock that surfaced was the roadblock caused by unresolved conflict between the grandparents and their own children. The number of reasons I could list as the causes for unresolved conflict between parents and their adult children are more than I have room to list; so instead of doing that I am simply going to say that one of the major roadblocks that grandparents face in becoming a spiritual influence in the lives of their grandchildren, is the fact that they have not made amends with their children over something that happened in the past. As one person shared with me years ago, "Failure to forgive or seek forgiveness for something you have done wrong is like drinking rat poison and expecting the rat to die."

- I often discover that there is resentment between the grandparents and their own kids. In my mind this is one of the biggest problems and often complicates all the other reasons they give.
- In conversation with the grandparents in our congregation the biggest challenge they face seems to be feelings of guilt over "having got it wrong" with their children. They now feel they can't do anything with their grandchildren because it would come across as hypocritical to their adult children.
- Many times the spiritual relationship between grandparents and their children is filled with spiritual hurt and neglect. In order for healing to take place, so that the door will open for a meaningful relationship between the grandparents and grandchildren, there must first be confession with repentance and forgiveness (see 2 Chronicles 7:14).

If you are familiar with the 12 Step program of Alcoholic Anonymous you would know that step number nine is known as the "making amends" step. When I preached a sermon series on the 12 Steps I phrased this step in the following way: "I must amend my relationships by forgiving those who have hurt me and seeking forgiveness from those I have hurt." The reality for many of you grandparents is the fact that if you want to be a spiritual influence in the lives of your grandchildren, you must first make amends with your adult children. You must either forgive or seek forgiveness before this roadblock can be busted!

Roadblock Busters

Since AA has been helping people make amends for years, I think the best advice I could give you comes from them. As my dad taught me from an early age, "Don't reinvent the wheel if you don't have to."

First, we will need to have the proper attitude as we approach this. It is good to have forgiven both ourselves and the people we injured, regardless of anything they might have done to retaliate. We will not succeed in resolving the conflict if we are still angry and defensive.

Second, we need to have a good idea going into the encounter about what we want to say and accomplish. Most importantly we want to make sure we state our apology without assigning any blame to the ones we injured. We must act responsibly as we make our confession and attempt amends, having

thought through all the possible consequences so that we will not be caught off
guard and be provoked to anger. A rehears-
al with a sponsor, therapist or friend may
help prepare us.

We need to be open to any response we
get from people we've injured, and be ready
to accept their response without becoming
angry. We are not there to manipulate them
into forgiving us. In order to have this come
off smoothly, we should make every effort
to purge our bad feelings toward the person
or incident before we meet to speak. This
will help us resist the temptation to point
out to them what we felt they did to pro-
voke us. We are only there to talk about our
own behaviour.

It is also a good idea not to take the
other person by surprise. They have a right
to know that you intend to make amends.
They have a right to refuse to let you do
so at this time. . . . You can leave an open
invitation to talk whenever and wherever
they might feel comfortable at some time
in the future.[1]

Grandparents, if you want to be an influence
in the lives of your grandchildren then you need
to be willing to do whatever it takes to restore and
reconcile the relationships you have with your adult

children. I think this 12 Step individual captures the attitude we are to have when he wrote:

> I make amends to those that I have harmed.
> I pay back debts I owe. I apologize. I write
> letters. I find time to do and say things that
> would help heal the damage that I have done.
> I try to bring goodness where previously I had
> brought discord and destruction. It takes in-
> sight, courage and dedication to make such
> amends, but now I have the help of my God
> to know what to do and how to do it. I learn
> to earnestly seek the right way to go about
> this process from my God. I start to live the
> kind of life that my God has meant for me
> to live all along.[2]

Roadblock #4—Busyness/Availability

Another common reason expressed for why grand-parents don't engage in the faith formation of their grandchildren, is the general busyness of their grand-children which prevents them from even having op-portunities to be with their grandchildren, much less be a spiritual influence in their lives. One Pastor shared,

> The number one thing I hear from grand-
> parents is that their kids and grandkids are
> largely inaccessible because their grandkids
> are too busy.

Roadblock Busters

There is no escaping the fact that we live in a fast-paced, do-anything-at-anytime culture which keeps families and children on the go. Yet, in spite of this, I still believe there is time for grandparents to be an influence in the lives of their grandchildren. The first thing I would recommend is that you "seize the times" rather than trying to "create a time."

My dad was a Bible camp director and one of the things he taught the counselors was to "seize teachable moments" which simply meant that when you see an opportunity to have a "God moment" or faith conversation, seize it. He felt those opportunities were more valuable than trying to get the kids to sit down for a formal Bible study. In the same way, as grandparents, you need to "seize the moments" God provides for you to have spiritual conversations or moments with your grandchildren rather than thinking you need to create some sort of spiritual time with your grandchildren. For example, when they are visiting you and a small thunderstorm rolls through that produces a rainbow, seize that opportunity to say, "Hey, everyone, look at that beautiful rainbow! By the way, what is that supposed to remind us of again?" Or if you are traveling in the minivan with them somewhere and you see an accident on the side of the road, seize the opportunity to ask them to pray with you for the people who were in the accident as well as the paramedics who are seeking to help.

A second roadblock buster is to simply create consistent times to spend with your grandchildren. One family I know has a regular Sunday dinner at the grandparents' home where they fix a meal and even go so far as to give $20 to each grandchild who attends, with the parent's permission of course. These Sunday afternoon dinners create opportunities for teachable moments for the grandparents. Another grandmother I knew, okay it was my mom, made sure that every summer when we are back in her area for vacation, that we go to the yellow ice cream shop together. It became a ritualistic time that we had together every summer. That visit to the yellow shop usually lasted at least two hours even though the ice cream shop was less than a mile away because it was our time to talk. We also made sure that we got together to celebrate Christmas every year but that took planning in order to accommodate what would work for all the families involved, it took place at all sorts of different times and in many locations. I remember one year we had to celebrate Christmas in July! It didn't matter because we still did it and it became another memory making time for us.

Yes our children and grandchildren are busy, but we can still seize the times we are given and create some ritualistic times that we get together to bust through this roadblock.

Roadblock #5–Feelings of Inadequacy

A final reason that surfaced was a general feeling of inadequacy that many grandparents have over the fact they feel out of touch with the things that their grandchildren are into:

> Many grandparents I work with don't feel like they have anything to offer. They are afraid of rejection in a day when their grandkids are crazy nuts on computers and social media, and the grandparents are scared of that world.

> I have tried to keep up with my grandkids and the technological whizz wig things they have and are into, but just when I seem to get one figured out it is already out of date, and I'm laughed at because they have moved on to the next version or thing. I want to connect with them but I don't want to look like a fool either, so I just find it easier to not even try.

If you are feeling inadequate as a grandparent it may bring you comfort to know that your adult children, in all likelihood, are feeling inadequate as parents as well. George Barna, in his book, *Revolutionary Parenting,* writes, "Consider that fewer than one out of every five parents of young children believe they are doing a good job of training their children morally and spiritually. In fact, when we asked a national sample of adults with children under eighteen to rate their parenting performance of fifteen different indicators, we discovered that parents ranked their efforts related to morality and spirituality at the bottom of the list."[3] So the good news for you as a grandparent is the fact that your feelings of inadequacy are probably matched by those of your adult children. They are just as uncertain and concerned about this as you are, so keep that in mind as you consider these roadblock busters.

Roadblock Busters

- *Become the student not the teacher. Turn your inadequacy into an opportunity:* Yes you feel inadequate and that's okay. Don't be ashamed of these feelings. In fact, you should share them with your grandchildren and use them as an opportunity to allow your grandchild to teach you something. My mom didn't know how to text, but she knew this was the way my daughter liked to communicate with others, so she asked my daughter to show her how, which she did. Later, when my daughter had a Facebook page, she asked my daughter to help her do the same thing so she could follow and interact with her granddaughter that way. While it became a little bit of a funny joke between us that my daughter would plan on the fact that when we visited Nana she would have to show her again how to use some sort of social media tool, it nonetheless became a bonding experience between grandma and granddaughter. My mom used her inadequacies as an opportunity to build a bond with her granddaughter.

- *Trust that God has given you experiences that are bigger than your inadequacies:* Remember that God has promised He will never give you more than you can handle, which means you have what you need to be the influence God wants you to be in the lives of your grandchildren. Trust in Him and the experiences he has given you which are more than adequate to be a spiritual influence in your grandchildren's lives. Don't let Satan's lies, that you are not good enough, ready enough, smart enough, restored enough or experienced enough to be a spiritual influence, convince you that you have nothing to offer. God would not give you something you couldn't handle.

So there you have it. The roadblocks and tools you need to overcome them so that you can be the Faith@Home Grandparent that God has called you to be.

DISCUSSION QUESTIONS

1. Which of the roadblocks do you face as a grandparent in being a spiritual influence in the lives of your grandchildren?

2. Which of the roadblock busters, for the roadblock(s) you face, did you find to be the most helpful and "doable?"

3. What actions steps are you going to take as a result of this chapter?

4. Are there any additional roadblocks that you face?

Notes

1. Claudette Wassi-Grimm, *The Twelve Step Journal* (New York: Overlook Press, 1999), p. 224-225.
2. From 12Step.org.
3. George Barna, *Revolutionary Parenting* (Carol Stream, IL: Tyndale House, 2010), p. 10.

Game Time

As I prepared to write this book I sent an e-mail out to some seniors I know, asking them to share ways they have found to "stay in the game" as spiritual influencers in the lives of their children and grandchildren. What you are going to read next are some of the testimonies, ideas and suggestions I received from them. If you want to look at more, or if you have something to add, please go to www.faithathome.com/grandparents and you will find a webpage of testimonies, ideas and resource recommendations along with a tab where you can add your testimony or idea.

From Dave and Linda Stegman

Hi Mark,

Being grandparents has been one of the biggest blessings of our lives. We see them at least once a week. We watch Samuel on Tuesday mornings so our daughter Robin can go to the women's Bible Study at her church.

I play children's Bible songs CDs when they are here and in the car and talk about the words. I like to use those times in the car (when there aren't other distractions) to talk about the Lord. For example, we talk about the trees changing with the seasons and how beautiful God has made our world. Going to a Christian school, our granddaughter, Elisabeth, has a memory verse to learn on a regular basis. I ask her to say it for me and then we discuss what it means. One time her verse was "fear not for I am with you" (Isaiah 41:10) and I asked her what she was afraid of. I think it was about being afraid of scary things in the dark and I reminded her that the verse promises she doesn't have to be afraid of the dark because God is always with her.

We think it's good to pray for "teachable moments" when we are with our grandchildren and not miss opportunities to share God's Word and spiritual truths with them.

We also feel that it's important to model prayer with our grandchildren by praying with them before each meal (even little Samuel folds his hands) as well as after reading a Bible story before bedtime. I want to pray for and with them more often and spontaneously, (such as when they fall or just to thank God and praise Him) to show them that they can talk to God anytime. Today when I was playing with Sammy, the Lord reminded me to place my hand on his head and pray (audibly) that he would become a "man after God's own heart" and be a mighty warrior for Him. Blessing and praying for our grandchildren to grow in their faith, asking Jesus to be their Lord and Savior, and for their future (friends, spouses, vocations, ministries and service to the Lord and others) is the most important thing we can do for them. It is the BEST gift we can give them, and that's coming from a grandmother who loves to buy gifts for her grandchildren!

I hope this helps, Mark. We will pray for you as you undertake this important work, that you will gather lots of good "advice" and thoughts, and most importantly, God's words and insights!

From Becky Danielson

My grandma was a prayer warrior for me. At 101 she woke up each day, prayed for each member of the family, including her great grands. She included each birthdate too, just to remind herself and keep her memory sharp. She ended her day the same way. I think there are fewer inhibitions with grandparents as well as a genuine desire to share faith with grandchildren. Bottom line, Mark, is love.

When one loves deeply and wants what's best for one's children and grandchildren, how can a person NOT talk about Jesus and pray earnestly for family members to come to Christ.

From Wanda Nelson Parker

I have found that sharing my own stories, my own struggles, have opened doors. On the first day of school this year I texted my 13-year-old granddaughter, Elsa, that I was praying for her. She texted me back with a question and we went back and forth until I got worried she was in class. Her last text was, "Thanks, Grammy, I really respect you, and your thoughts are important to me." I just had cancer surgery two weeks ago and spent the first few days after leaving the hospital in their home. I had one day that was really horrible and Elsa was my "babysitter." She sat on the couch and cried with me and prayed for me.

I think it is about being vulnerable. Maybe that should begin with being vulnerable with our children so they will trust us with their children.

From Earl and Char Wintz

None of our 15 grandchildren (ages 10 to 34) live very close. However, with e-mail, Skype,

Facebook, phone, etc., it's easy to touch base with them in a minimal way. We, being old fashioned, think a letter is much more special: it's private and can be tucked away to read another time.

Practical things we have done include:

- Attend church regularly as a family
- We both have been on boards/committees and still are—and we tell "kids" about these and other interesting activities at our church.
- All five of our children also attended Bible camps with our church.
- We read from the Bible as a family every morning and take turns saying grace before meals and also sing the Doxology before dinner, when they are with us. These practices are being repeated by our children for our grandchildren and on to our four great grandchildren.
- Char has a big platter of cookies or fudge on the table when they visit.
- I always have some fix-it jobs to do or some project. They all have developed a healthy work ethic.
- On visits, Char has the younger ones set the table with flowers, candles, etc.
- Our oldest daughter and family worked for a mission organization

for six years in Ghana. The others went on short-term mission trips helping with projects in their churches.

- We would often sing together when riding along in the car. They are all musically capable. The boys each play guitars.

We would like to visit our "kids" more in person, but instead we have to make it up with the old and new communication media. Write short letters and include clippings, Scripture and prayer requests. I hope these ideas help. May the Lord enable and guide you!

From Linda Antle Ranson Jacobs

Last year when my daughter was deployed to Afghanistan we moved from NC to FL to live with my son-in-law and help with our three grandsons. I became their spiritual leader at that point. What engaged me to invest in their spiritual lives was the permission of my daughter and my son-in-law. They welcomed it, which made it easier for me. To pray with the littlest one when his mom was gone over the holidays was beyond special. To minister to the teen during teen crisis times brought a sense of intimacy between a teen grandson and his grandmother. And to teach the third grader about Bible stories and how they relate to our lives . . . well . . . I don't even have the words.

From Julie Holmen

I'm not a grandparent, but my grandfather (Mom's dad) is still a spiritual influence in my life, even though he went to Heaven over 40 years ago. Being a very young observer of what he made a priority in his life (his God, his church, his family, his integrity); listening to the guidance he gave me (be patient with others and yourself, know you are a cherished child of God; take time to enjoy God's creation; be kind and compassionate to others); learning how he conducted himself while fighting in the war (carrying a friend for miles while on a march as captives so that his injured friend wouldn't be shot; enjoying the beauty of the French countryside and the kindness of its people even while waiting to go to the front lines). He is still a spiritual influence for all these reasons, and because of the faith he imbedded in his daughter and three sons who, in turn, modeled their strong faith for us throughout their lives. Grandfather is a testament to passing along a love for God by teaching it and modeling it in every large and small aspect of his life.

MARK HOLMEN

One of the simplest—but deeply touching ways—that his daughter saw his faith (and I got to witness a few times myself) was watching him step out onto the back steps of their farmhouse every morning, without fail (no matter what worries were on his mind or what struggles he knew he faced that day) and whistling to the birds. He always wanted to start his day by appreciating the blessings of life God had given and to quietly teach his children and grandchildren that no matter what, God is in control and all is well.

From Linda Weddle
(*Faith@Home Grandparents* Blog Writer)

The Happy Table

On a typical March day, misty air floated over a waiting-for-first-signs-of-spring landscape. By suppertime the day's dreariness was in danger of infiltrating my brain. The solution? Getting my two granddaughters and heading for the local Chinese restaurant. We would create some fun on this dismal day. I ordered the chicken chow mein and they ordered their usual mountain of fried rice. Then I prayed, thanking the Lord for the privilege of being a grandmother to such fantastic kids. As we dug in, I asked them about their day and what they had been learning in school.

They told me about a party they had attended and then we got into a discussion as to whether or not God ever needs to say "goodbye." (Kid theological discussions are fascinating.)

But, their spiritual training is not dependent on me. Both my children married Christian spouses and are raising their children in Christ-centered environments. Yet that doesn't mean I don't have responsibility. I am back-up support to their parents. I am a question-answerer, verse-memorizer helper and sometimes biblical-concept explainer. Just as we prayed that our own children would grow up with an intentional desire to make their multitude of daily decisions with a godly perspective, so I pray the same for my grandchildren.

"Grandma," the younger one interrupts my thoughts, "do you think we'll get fortune cookies?"

"Probably," I say and then I look at her wide-eyed and puzzled, "but how will we know whose is whose?"

Now all three of us know (really we do) that fortune cookies don't mean anything, but I pretend to take it seriously. "Maybe you'll get mine and I'll get yours," I tell her. Just then the server rather unceremoniously drops three fortune cookies on the table. "See," I look worried. "Just imagine if your fortune says something about your job. You don't have a job. I have a job."

As I seriously continue discussing the conundrum of mixed-up fortune cookies, our giggles get louder and louder and I see people staring at us. So I dole out the cookies. The younger one opens hers up and is suddenly laughing and crying all at the same time. "Look," she says, thrusting the paper toward me. "I did get the wrong one." I read. "You'll have a good day at the office tomorrow." We are now all three in hysterics. Across from us two businessmen get up from their dinner. The one heads to the counter to pay the bill and the other walks toward our table. "Oh, no," I think. "We made too much noise." But what he says is, "I wish I had been sitting here tonight. This was the happy table."

Ahhh . . . a memorable moment because isn't that exactly what I desire? That my grandchildren know me as a person . . .

. . . who very much loves the Lord

. . . who very much loves them

And that when we're together . . . we're at the happy table.

From Myrne Holmen
(written just a few weeks before she went to be with the Lord)

I couldn't think of my role as a grandparent, without thinking of my grandparents.

One set of grandparents passed away before I was born. I have one memory of my Grandpa Current when he was still alive. My parents had dropped me off at my grandparents' home, while they went to spend the day at the county fair. I thought it was great until evening, when I started to wonder when my parents would be back. I sat in my little rocking chair and my grandfather in his chair—my grandfather looking imposing, tall, slender and with a well-groomed mustache.

He reassured me that my parents would be coming. But soon, he could tell I was a little more anxious and he invited me to sit on his lap until they came. Why would this be the one memory I had? I think it is because, along with the fun of the day, he offered me love and security for a few minutes when I was afraid.

I think one of the most difficult things about being a grandparent, is learning to have "little bits" of love, when we are willing to give and receive so much more. I'm sure my grandfather would have treasured more time to share his love with me. But when my parents came, they were my world and everything was okay. Those "little bits" of love from my grandfather became a treasure that has lasted my lifetime. How blessed are we to have had grandparents and to be grandparents.

5

Even If They Stray, You Stay

I am privileged to have the opportunity to travel all over the world leading Extreme Faith@Home Makeover parenting seminars where I motivate and equip parents to reestablish the following Faith@Home behaviors in their home:

- *Faith Talk*—Seizing everyday opportunities to have faith conversations with our children so God is talked about throughout the week and not simply on Sunday mornings.
- *Prayer*—Maintaining an open and honest dialogue to and with Jesus at mealtime, bedtime, morning time and even in the car through prayer.
- *Bible Reading*—Making sure that the Bible is the most prominent and read book in our homes because it is so much more than a book; it's the living Word of God!

- *Service*—Engaging with our children in random acts of kindness as well as community service and some sort of global missions.
- *Boundaries and Discipline*—Setting clear boundaries for what is acceptable and what is not and affirming positive behavior as well as following through with the discipline for inappropriate behavior.

The seminars are always filled with a lot of energy, interaction, positivity as many practical ideas are shared that leave everyone feeling that these things are very doable. As I conclude the seminar the Lord has led me to make this final point and challenge which I would like to share with you as well.

I wish I could guarantee you that if you do all the above listed things with your children and grandchildren it would mean they would never stray or walk away from their faith in Jesus Christ. Unfortunately, I can't guarantee that because I have experienced many parents and grandparents in my life who have done everything right and yet their children and/or grandchildren have strayed. I have faced many parents who have come to me completely distraught over the actions and behaviors of their teenager or young adult child asking, "What did we do wrong? We brought them to church, we prayed and read the Bible with them at home and they used to be so into their faith and now they don't want anything to do with us or God. What are we supposed to do?"

The pain, fear, worries and frustration in them is strong as their stomach is in knots and their hearts are broken.

I would then remind them the story of the prodigal son (see Luke 15:11-32) where I would begin by saying, "There was a mom and dad who were like you in the fact that they did everything right with their two sons. They brought them to church, personally taught them the ways of God, read the Scriptures to them and lived their lives in faithful service to God. When their boys became teenagers one of their sons didn't want anything to do with them or their lifestyle anymore. In fact, he wanted out all together. He didn't want anything to do with church, faith, God, the family or the family business and he became very disrespectful. In fact he was so disrespectful that he went to his dad and asked if he could have the money that he was designated to get when his father died. Now that's pretty disrespectful but it just shows how far off the deep end this teenager had gone. This is not what I'm recommending by any means, but the father gave his son his inheritance and the son left.

"The story follows the son and what happens to him which is somewhat to be expected as he blows through the money partying and winds up hitting rock bottom feeding pigs just to survive. Eventually the son realizes he could make a better living working for his father so he decides to go home but instead of looking at the son, who is the primary character in the story, I want you to look at the supporting actor in the story; the father. What did he do while his son was straying? He stayed. He stayed committed to his faith, his God, and his business and his God-honoring lifestyle. As far as I'm concerned that deserves a Best Supporting Actor nomination because he stayed faithfully committed to God even when his son was straying. And please keep in mind, that story takes place at a time where there were no cell phones or Facebook pages. As far as this father knew his son had left and was probably dead. *And still* this father remained committed to God and living his life for Him. And why is that so significant? Why does that deserve a nomination? Because when his son needed a place to come home to where was the father? Right there in the same place, with the same faith, ready and willing to welcome him back with no judgment or scorn but with a celebration instead!"

As grandparents you probably have one child or grandchild who is your prodigal and that is not easy for you. You desperately want them to come back to Christ but at this point you don't know if they ever will and that is tearing you up inside. My encouragement to you is to make sure you stay as they stray so they have a place to come home to when they need it. Don't give up on them and don't give up on God. And while I can't confirm this, I can make an educated guess that the father in this story would have drawn some of his strength to stay from the words of the Shema, which he would have memorized and recited many times with his children:

These are the commands, decrees and laws the LORD your God directed me to teach you to observe in the land that you are crossing the Jordan to possess, so that you, your children and their children after them may fear the LORD your God as long as you live by keeping all his decrees and commands that I give you, and so that you may enjoy long life. Hear, O Israel, and be careful to obey so that it may go well with you and that you may increase greatly in a land flowing with milk and honey, just as the LORD, the God of your fathers, promised you. Hear, O Israel: The LORD our God, the LORD is one. Love the LORD your God with all your heart and with all your soul and with all your strength. These commandments that I give you today are to be upon your hearts. Impress them on your children. Talk about them when you sit at home and when you walk along the road, when you lie down and when you get up. Tie them as symbols on your hands and bind them on your foreheads. Write them on the doorframes of your houses and on your gates (Deuteronomy 6:1-9).

If you have a child or grandchild who is straying, here is how I would preach that passage to you.

1. Trust in the commands, decrees, laws and promises of God. You know them. You know

that God loves your children and knows them even better than you do as God even knows every hair on their head and has them numbered! God doesn't want them to perish anymore than you do. Therefore, you need to trust that God has a plan and is at work in ways we cannot know, see or understand. Trust and take comfort in the fact that God's plan is for you, your children and your children's children to spend all eternity together enjoying life with Him!

2. Listen up, now is a time when *you* need to be careful because Satan wants to use this difficult time to get you off the rails as well. You need to continue to obey and follow God remaining committed to your relationship with Him. Don't turn from God or blame Him for this and don't let guilt paralyze or defeat you. Yes your kids or grandchildren are straying right now and that breaks your heart, but you need not to give up on them or God right now. As you know well, you can't control your kids or grandchildren, but the one thing you can control is you, so keep on praying, keep on reading the Word, worshipping and giving your life in service to Him. And be ever ready to welcome them when they come home!

3. And listen up, stay in love with God through this. Love him with all of your heart, soul and strength through this time because that enduring and growing love you have for God will leave an impression on your children and children's children. Don't be ashamed about your love for God and when given the opportunity, talk openly and honestly about it. And finally, make sure your home and lifestyle reflect the love you have for Christ so while they may not have it themselves, they can certainly see what a loving relationship with God looks like.

As a pastor, I had an opportunity to conduct numerous funeral or memorial services for grandparents I knew who had children or grandchildren who were straying at the time. I had heard about these "prodigals" by name but in many cases my first time meeting them would take place at the service. While they would seem somewhat disinterested in me or the church, you could see that the service for their grandparent impacted them through the testimonies that were shared about their love and commitment to Christ. Over my years as a pastor I was able to see many of these prodigals come home to Christ and in most cases they would testify to the fact that it was their grandparent's faith that compelled them to come home. As one prodigal shared with me in an e-mail:

Pastor Mark, I wish my grandma could see that I'm right with God again. I know there wasn't a day that she wasn't praying for me to give God another chance and yet I was so mean and disrespectful to her through the years for continually pushing God on me and yet she never stopped, changed or gave up on me. I will never forget her funeral service as it rocked me pretty hard even though I didn't want to admit it at the time. Finally, I realized if I wanted what she had which was peace, hope, joy and purpose then I needed to do what she did and give my life to Christ. I know she's in heaven cheering me on but I look forward to the day when I can celebrate this with her.

The longer you remain a grandparent, or the more times you become a grandparent, the likelier it becomes that you will have a prodigal in your life. When that happens we need to trust in the promises of God, be careful that we don't let this take us off course and remain in a loving relationship with Christ so that God can work through us to bring them home. If we aren't careful and don't remain, then we close ourselves to the opportunity of being used by God to bring them home. I know that is the last thing you would want to do. Some of you will have a chance to see them come home while you are still here on earth. Others of you will see it happen from your home in heaven. But in either case there will be great rejoicing!

Faith@Home Grandparents Idea

One church I know of decided to create a "Prodigal Wall" which was a billboard sized space in their lobby. The Prodigal Wall provided a place where you could write the name of a prodigal on a sheet of paper and thumbtack it to the side of the wall that had images of the world on it. The seniors Sunday School class took it upon themselves to pray for those names every week. When a prodigal came home, back to Christ, his or her name was moved to the other side of the wall where there was a picture depicting a heavenly home. When a prodigal came home that name and story was also shared during the announcements at the services and the entire congregation would applaud. As the pastor shared with me, "We didn't want to hide the fact that many of us have prodigals. In fact the first name to go on the wall was my son's name. We had no idea how many people had prodigals, but the healing that happened simply by posting their names on the wall was amazing. Many were ashamed of the fact that they had prodigals but they were able to get rid of the shame by posting their children's names on the wall. And then when a prodigal comes home and we announce it in church, not only is it fun to celebrate, but it's like the rest of us all get renewed hope for our sons and daughters. When my son came home it was probably the best day in my entire ministry career."

Faith@Home grandparents stay even if/when their children and/or grandchildren stray.

DISCUSSION QUESTIONS

1. Were you or someone in your family, a prodigal? What was that like? What brought you/them home?
2. Do you have any prodigals in your family? Please share the story if you are willing.
3. What is the hardest part of being the parent or grandparent of a prodigal?
4. What is something you can do, as a grandparent, for your prodigal?

Acknowledgments

I want to thank all of the grandparents who have attended my seminars and shared their thoughts, encouragement and ideas with me for Faith@Home: Grandparents. I truly couldn't have done this without you. I also want to thank all the good people at Gospel Light and Regal Books who continue to believe in the importance of the Faith@Home movement and message. Their willingness to produce this book along with all the other resources we have done over the years shows their commitment. I couldn't ask for a better publisher and I am so thankful that God brought me to Ventura in 2002 and into a relationship with Gospel Light—this was clearly a part of God's plan. And finally, I want to thank everyone who has helped and continues to help me recover from the sudden and tragic loss of my mom. She and I had talked about her joining me for some Faith@Home grandparenting seminars, which I know she would have loved to do. While that is no longer possible, I know her spirit will be with me. And out of the broken glass pieces produced by the pain of losing my mom, God is putting together a new stained glass picture. My family and I are moving to Crosslake, Minnesota to take over possession of my parent's home and to base our ministry there where the MJH Faith@Home Ministry Center that has been established and dedicated in her name.

MARK HOLMEN

MARK A. HOLMEN

To find out more about Mark Holmen's
speaking engagements and to learn more about
the Faith@Home movement, visit faithathome.com.
Mark is available to speak to parents and church
leaders about how to be a faith-at-home focused
individual, family and church. For more information,
please contact Mark at mark@faithathome.com.

Also by Mark Holmen

Faith Begins @Home Prayer

Faith Begins @Home Devotions

Faith Begins @Home Dad

Faith Begins @Home Family

Faith Begins @Home Mom

Available wherever books are sold!

In Whose Footsteps Will Your Children Follow?

In the past, faith was a central part of the family's home life, passed on from generation to generation. Today, the reality for many families is that faith is no more than one-hour, drop-off Christianity, if it is present at all. What does this mean for the faith of our children? How will they come to know Christ? And how does a family put Christ at the center of their busy lives?

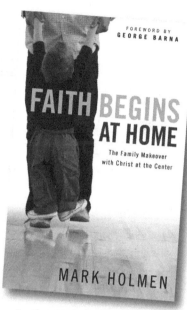

Mark Holmen knows that becoming the strong, healthy, joy-filled families God intended begins with parents establishing their homes as the primary place where faith is nurtured. In this engaging book, you will learn about the importance of your walk with the Lord; and of the role the church should play with families. Filled with a wealth of practical ideas, inspirational stories and biblical truths, *Faith Begins at Home* will inspire, motivate and equip you to help your family succeed.

Faith Begins at Home • Mark Holmen

Available wherever books are sold!